Unleash Your Inner Money Babe

Uplevel Your Money Mindset and Manifest $1,000 In 21 Days.

A MONEY MANIFESTING WORKBOOK
BY KATHRIN ZENKINA

Unleash Your Inner Money Babe

DISCLAIMER:

Dedication

To my parents who supported me relentlessly through the many years of not knowing what I wanted to do with my life; to Brennan who watched the birth of this book, my company, and who held my hand the entire way; to my Manifestation Babes who urged me to keep going all those days that I felt like giving up; to my team for helping this book become a reality and serve thousands of women to come; to Stephanie for igniting my entrepreneurial passion and being my biggest support system when I didn't have one; and to you, the reader, for committing to raising the vibration of this planet with me and spreading the truth about money. I couldn't do it without you.

Contents

Introduction

Hello, Gorgeous Soul!

Congratulations on saying "yes" to an exciting new journey and taking on a money manifesting challenge unlike any other. I am so freaking excited about the journey that is ahead of you. I am literally sitting here smiling as I write this knowing the incredible money mindset transformation that is right up ahead of you.

I strongly believe that our paths crossed for a reason. *Something* told you that this was your next step, and you took massive action by purchasing this book. I am so incredibly proud of you already for finding yourself in a book like this. You are 100% ready to unleash your inner Money Babe.

Get ready for some amazing, much needed, life changing, mind blowing money mindset shifts that are going to happen over the next 21 days.

Who am I and why did I create the Money Babe challenge?

My name is Kathrin Zenkina and I am a spiritual mindset coach and creator of the Manifestation Babe™ brand. It is my life purpose and mission to empower you to breakthrough your limitations, up level your life, and manifest a reality wilder than your wildest dreams. I, also, strongly believe that I was put on this planet to teach you the truth about money.

I created this 21-day challenge because I got really tired of watching other women undercharge, under earn, drown themselves in money related misery, and give into complete bullshit messaging when it comes to money.

Society has totally and completely misled us. As a result, we have developed the most ridiculous, self-limiting, and outrageously crazy beliefs when it comes to this "taboo" topic.

Either you were raised to believe that money is the root of all evil, you experienced never having enough money your entire life, you're struggling with making ends meet right now and don't know why, or you've got plenty of the green stuff but you're feeling guilty for your success.

Whatever stage you're at, you need help. You're over this ickiness when it comes to your finances. You're ready to drop the struggle.

I get you 100%. As most of us, I was there too. Thankfully, we can change this ASAP.

I started my money mindset journey $25,000 in debt earning just about $400 a week. I was overwhelmed, stressed, frustrated, and frantic when it came to thinking about, talking about, earning, or spending money. Money was a source of major stress for me.

I have a pretty good idea of how you feel, and I feel called to help you. Thus, the Universe conspired to have me write this book and you to pick it up and read it.

My sole goal over the next 21 days is to help you manifest (*yes, manifest*) your very first $1,000 to prove to yourself it can be done. I want to show you that it's more than possible to bring more money into your bank account, drop the money struggle, and not even know exactly "how" the extra money is going to show up.

It sounds crazy, but I do it all the time. So do my clients.

Money doesn't have to be hard. Money doesn't have to remain a mystery anymore. It's not evil. It doesn't make you a bad person, and it certainly doesn't have a mind of its own. Money is something we can get really comfortable with. And I'm ready to share all my secrets with you.

Why are we manifesting $1,000?

The better question is, why are we *only* manifesting $1,000?

I believe $1,000 is a great starting goal especially for the money manifesting newbie, so let's just go with it. You can set your money manifesting goal to any amount. It can be $100, or $100,000 in the 21-day period. The amount is totally up to you. For the sake of the challenge, let's focus on bringing in $1,000. The *only* limit to what you end up manifesting is what you *believe* you can manifest. You might be someone who just doesn't see the possibility yet, and that's ok. That was me before I started my money manifesting journey. I didn't realize how much I was limiting myself simply by not believing that it was possible.

I didn't think I was good enough, smart enough, or responsible enough to make it happen. I didn't feel like I deserved it either. Does that sound familiar? If yes, then this book was made for you.

Over the next 21 days, I will be equipping you with daily assignments I call "money babe actions" that pertain to your money mindset in a workbook format. As you'll soon notice, there will be plenty of space for you to take notes, answer questions, and work out each assignment. This will help you keep yourself accountable and make it way more fun than just reading a book on money.

I want to help you take action, babe.

You may have the urge to skip ahead and read all 21 days at once. Being someone who gets really excited about new adventures, I completely understand you. However, I urge you to take it one day at a time and not skip ahead until it's time. Take the time to work through each of the money babe actions as *these* will be the game changers of each lesson. Trust me, you'll get so much more out of this challenge if you take it one day at a time.

The assignments will range from 10-30 minutes a day. The time you spend on this journey is your *only* energetic investment in order to receive your money from the amazing, unlimited, and mind-blowing Universe.

Sounds pretty sweet, doesn't it?

Keep in mind, I will *not* be touching upon the who/what/when/where/why of manifestation and all the other lengthy details.

I did this on purpose because I'm pretty sure you've had your fair share of watching *The Secret* and diving into countless other self-help books on the basics of Law of Attraction. Instead of boring you with the details, I'd rather jump right into the fun.

However, if you're someone who *really* wants to know all the details of *why* you're doing something before you set your mind to it, then I invite you to take an adventure and do a little bit of googling. There are countless books, courses, articles, and blog posts on the science behind manifesting and it's truly fascinating. Keep in mind that knowing all the details is completely optional. Just like the forces behind gravity and electricity still work whether or not you understand the science behind it, the same goes for the principles I will be sharing with you over the next 21 days.

If you need the quickest explanation of the Law of Attraction, think "like attracts like." Positive energy is attracted to positive thoughts, emotions, and feelings. Negative energy is attracted to negative thoughts, emotions, and feelings. Think shitty thoughts, feel shitty feelings, and you'll manifest a shitty reality. Think radiant thoughts, feel radiant feelings, and you'll manifest a radiant reality. Your outer reality is an exact reflection of your inner reality. There really is nothing more to know for now, as you will learn a *lot* more as we go through the daily money babe actions together.

When I first started my money manifesting journey, I was able to manifest $2,000 in a 21-day period following this exact challenge that I have created. Nowadays, it's not uncommon at all for me to manifest over $200,000 in a 30-day period, month after month.

I've had students manifest $6,000 in 7 days, $1,000 in a single day, or $10,000 in the 21-day period. Let's just say I've seen it all. There are no limits except for the ones that you create for yourself. You can manifest any amount that you *believe* you can manifest.

I am *so* excited to get started. Are you?!

Before we begin Day One, I just have a few pre-challenge questions for you. Take a few minutes to go inward, dig deep for the answers, and see what comes up. This will help you prepare for the next 21 days.

Money Babe Action

1. Why are you here? What inspired you to start this journey?

_____

_____

_____

2. What are you ready to shift when it comes to your finances?

_____

_____

_____

3. What is it that made you say "enough is enough?"

_____

_____

_____

4. On a scale of 1-10, how committed are you to radically transforming your money story over the next 21 days?

_____

_____

_____

5. How would it feel to manifest an extra $1,000 within the next 21-day period?

_____

_____

_____

6. What would you do with the money and why?

_____

_____

_____

7. When do you plan to sit down, open up each lesson, and do the necessary work required? Commitment is key here! Give an exact time of day.

_____

_____

_____

Day One

CLEARING OUT THE CRAP

Welcome to Day One, Gorgeous!

Are you ready to get the money manifesting party started? Me too!

Day one is all about clearing the unnecessary crap and clutter we don't realize is interfering with our finances.

Although eventually it's in your best interest to get organized in every single aspect of your daily life, don't worry about spring cleaning everything in sight in a single day. That would be too overwhelming and I want this to be an easy and fun process.

Why is today about clearing the crap and the clutter? Because money is just pieces of paper with energy attached to it. Energy needs space to flow. So if your surroundings are cluttered with crap left and right, then it's no wonder money isn't finding you!

I want you to remember this: Money is just energy and you have the power to direct the energy to you. By clearing out space, you make room for more energy to flow around you and to you. Makes sense, right?

Alright, I know what you're thinking. You may find pretty quickly that this book is filled with a bit of woo-woo and energy talk. Depending on where you are in your manifesting journey, you may either be used to it or think it's really weird.

Before your eyes roll too far in the back of your head, think of it this way. I once heard a quote that stuck with me from a book called "Secrets of the Millionaire Mind," by T. Harv Eker. In his book, that's highly recommended by the way, he said (and allow me to paraphrase) "I'd rather be really weird and really rich, than really cool and really broke!" I don't remember precisely word for word the *exact* quote, but it went something like that. If it works, it freaking works. Just go with it. You can go back to your old ways in 21 days if that feels better for you. But after being $1,000 richer, I guarantee you won't want to.

For today's money babe action, I want you to completely clear out your wallet, one area where you deal with money (the place where you pay your bills, keep bills, keep receipts, your laptop if you have an online business, etc.), and pick one extra space you spend the most time in.

Beginning with your wallet, I want you to toss out any old receipts, old used up gift cards, gum wrappers, and other miscellaneous items that serve no purpose in your wallet.

If you have any dollar bills in there right now, I want you to make sure they are not crumpled up. Straighten them out and sort them by size with the largest bill always facing you first. I find that when I have my $100 bills facing me first, I feel way more abundant than looking at a $1 bill first.

If you have no bills in there, feel free to put a $100 bill in there for the sake of raising your money vibe. Trust me, it feels really good to open your wallet every time you pay for something and see a crisp Benjamin looking right back at you. Hey there, fella!

Over the time, I've spent studying money and manifesting an abundance of it, I noticed that really abundant, wealthy, and successful people *respect* their money. Not surprisingly at all, money respects them in return. If someone crumpled you up and put you into a tiny space, you wouldn't be too happy either. Keeping your wallet clean and organized invites in more money.

Do the same with the area where you deal with your money (like possibly your office, kitchen counter, a table in your house, etc.) and that extra space you spend the most time in. It could be your car, your living room, your bedroom, your closet, or anywhere else.

Another way to promote the flow of energy in the areas of your choice is to buy some sage and burn it in these places. Run the smoke through your wallet, in your office, and wherever else you choose to organize. Sage is known to clear out old, stale, stagnant, negative energy. You can find sage in any metaphysical store or even on Amazon! I'm known to have a regular shipment of sage as I am pretty much addicted to the stuff. Clearing negativity is kinda my thing.

Now that we cleared out the crap, let me mention one more thing. In order for this 21-day journey to work, you have to *believe* it will. Any doubt you feed into your daily money babe actions will cause you to halt your manifesting progress. Doubt is the easiest way to direct your life straight to mediocrity. I am here to help you break this life sucking cycle. We're gonna practice having faith.

You know you've heard people say "I'll believe it when I'll see it" at some point in your life. Well, here's the truth that I want you to know. That's just not how the Universe works. It's actually when you BELIEVE it, that you will SEE it. You are the co-creator of your very own reality. You have to believe it works first before it works. So just go with it.

Believe with every little bit of you that by the end of the 21 days, you will manifest your $1,000. Start to expect it. Get excited about it right now. Celebrate it because it's already on its way to you *right now* as we speak.

Once you're done with clearing out the three spaces, answer the following money babe action questions.

Money Babe Action

1. How do you feel about your wallet now that it's cleaned out and cleared of things that don't belong in there?

_____

_____

_____

2. Did you make any discoveries hiding in your wallet? Many babes have reported forgotten gift cards, hidden cash, and other little goodies hiding under all the mess.

_____

_____

_____

3. Which area do you handle most of your finances in?

_____

4. How does it feel to have that area organized, cleaned out, and ready to receive more money?

5. What was the other area you chose that you spend the most time in?

6. How do you feel now that it's cleaned out and all the clutter is gone? Lighter? Happier? Able to breathe easier?

_____

_____

7. Did you buy sage and smoke it through these areas? If so, do you feel like the negative energy has been broken up?

_____

_____

_____

8. Did you make any other awesome discoveries today?

_____

_____

_____

Notes:

Day Two

The F Word Will Set You Free

Congratulations on clearing out physical space in your life for good energy to flow freely and easily into your life.

Are you ready to do part two of clearing?

What? More clearing?

Today is about doing some super crucial mental clearing. Day two may change your life alone. You could literally stop the challenge after day two and I guarantee you will see some major shifts in your life. However, I know you're an overachiever and eager to manifest $1,000. So, let's continue.

I have seen today's money babe action be the breakthrough moment for so many of my students and private clients. For me personally, it was *the* manifestation game changer, and at the time I didn't even realize it.

Today is the day to completely forgive yourself, everyone in your past, and everything that has ever happened to you since your birth. I know it sounds like a huge daunting task ahead of you, and you may be thinking "Forgive everyone?! Kathrin, do you even know what so-and-so did to me in 2004?!"

And I am here to tell you that it doesn't matter what so-and-so did to you. What truly matters is that holding onto *any* grudges from your past is going to prevent you from manifesting money.

Forgiving someone doesn't mean that they never did anything wrong. Forgiving someone means that you love yourself enough to let go of the shitty situation that no longer serves you. It's time to allow yourself some relief and open yourself up to more magic in your life.

Holding onto a grudge is the equivalent of intending to poison someone, but ending up drinking the poison yourself. Just like physical junk has been clogging up your wallet and your money spaces, the mental junk is clogging up your precious heart. Even if you think you let go of past negative situations, they may still live within you in your precious heart space. The way to release it all is to forgive it all.

Today's money babe action is a powerful one.

I want you to create a list of situations, people, and events that you know deep inside you must forgive. This list should contain anything that has had a negative impact on your life in one way or another. Be sure to look for situations that tie to money, but feel free to go beyond that. In the end, as I've mentioned before, money is just energy. Doing anything to unblock the flow of energy will attract more money into your life.

This is something that a lot of other money gurus won't tell you because they want you to believe that there are *specific* money manifesting secrets you have to follow or you'll manifest anything *but* money. Just know that the more positivity you add into your life, the more good energy you attract, resulting in more money. Law of attraction works the same way whether
you are manifesting a cup of coffee or a million dollars. Got it?

Good!

We'll get into plenty of money specific strategies later, but you'll also learn that money specific manifestations will also help you increase other manifestations as well. It's all intertwined. It's all just *energy*. To give you an idea of what I'm looking for, allow me to share with you a sample of my personal forgiveness list that I wrote down when I first started my journey.

Kathrin's Money Forgiveness List:

1. The time when I really wanted to buy a certain Barbie, and my mom told me that we couldn't afford it.

2. The time when I told my friends I was going to start a business and they laughed at me and told me that it wasn't a great idea because I'd surely fail.

3. The one time my boyfriend emotionally cheated on me with one of his coworkers.

4. That one time I cheated on my boyfriend because I was bored with our relationship.

5. The time when my best friend ruined one of my favorite t-shirts and didn't tell me about it until I found out myself.

6. The one time at the grocery store when my credit card was maxed out and I couldn't afford my groceries and had to put everything back. SO embarrassing.

7. The one time that I asked for a raise and didn't get one.

The goal here is to keep going and going until you can't think of anything else. I want you to try and find at least 20-25 situations that you remember from your past that involved a negative experience of some sort. No matter how small and silly some of them may seem, write it down. As you have noticed reading some of my own examples, some of the situations are laughable. The Barbie seems so unimportant in my life today as an adult, but taking a closer look, that was the first time in my life I heard the phrase "we can't afford it." This led to me growing up thinking that money was a limited resource and hard to come by.

Even though I now know that money is abundant and there are trillions of dollars flowing around me at any point in time, I wouldn't have believed it if I didn't first release and forgive the source of my opposing limiting belief.

Once you have written out your list, I want you to go back, re-read each situation and really feel the feelings you felt at the time it happened. Feeling is a powerful way to quickly discover what you need to release, and you will certainly find that there is a lot more negative energy tied to each situation than you initially thought. This is why we are doing this work. We need to clear up any negative energy so that we stop attracting similar experiences into our lives. After you dwell for like 2 seconds on the feelings you had in the moment of each of those situations, I want you to say *out loud* to each situation: "I forgive you. I'm sorry. Thank you. I love you." And I want you to truly mean it.

At the time, I started to do this, I didn't realize that what I was doing is actually an ancient Hawaiian practice for healing called "Ho'oponopono". It's super effective and works magic in forgiveness.

The meaning behind each phrase is this:

"I forgive you" = I will release this from myself and it is no longer my problem. I will no longer allow this situation to affect me and block my money vibe.

"I'm sorry" = I acknowledge the situation and I am sorry for holding onto it for so long. It will no longer be allowed to bother me.

"Thank you" = Thank you for all the lessons that this situation taught me

"I love you" = Sending love to the situation will allow you to heal and get through it. Everything is accomplished with love.

After doing this money babe action, you may discover that you will feel much lighter. You will feel like you have literally cleared out space in your heart for more good energy to flow in.

Continue to practice forgiveness on a daily basis. Forgiveness alone will completely revolutionize your life and daily behaviors in general. Next time someone hurts you or cuts you off in traffic, you can forgive them right away instead of holding onto a grudge for the rest of the day.

Say it with me: The more I forgive, the more at peace I will be. The more at peace I am, the more of my divine abundance freely flows to me.

Money Babe Action

Create your forgiveness list:

1.

_____

I FORGIVE YOU. I'M SORRY. THANK YOU. I LOVE YOU.

2.

_____

I FORGIVE YOU. I'M SORRY. THANK YOU. I LOVE YOU.

3.

_____

I FORGIVE YOU. I'M SORRY. THANK YOU. I LOVE YOU.

4.

_____

I FORGIVE YOU. I'M SORRY. THANK YOU. I LOVE YOU.

5.

_____

I FORGIVE YOU. I'M SORRY. THANK YOU. I LOVE YOU.

6.

_____

I FORGIVE YOU. I'M SORRY. THANK YOU. I LOVE YOU.

7.

_____

I FORGIVE YOU. I'M SORRY. THANK YOU. I LOVE YOU.

8.

_____

I FORGIVE YOU. I'M SORRY. THANK YOU. I LOVE YOU.

9.

_____

I FORGIVE YOU. I'M SORRY. THANK YOU. I LOVE YOU.

10.

_____

I FORGIVE YOU. I'M SORRY. THANK YOU. I LOVE YOU.

11.

_____

I FORGIVE YOU. I'M SORRY. THANK YOU. I LOVE YOU.

12.

_____

I FORGIVE YOU. I'M SORRY. THANK YOU. I LOVE YOU.

13.

_____

I FORGIVE YOU. I'M SORRY. THANK YOU. I LOVE YOU.

14.

_____

I FORGIVE YOU. I'M SORRY. THANK YOU. I LOVE YOU.

15.

_____

I FORGIVE YOU. I'M SORRY. THANK YOU. I LOVE YOU.

16.

_____

I FORGIVE YOU. I'M SORRY. THANK YOU. I LOVE YOU.

17.

_____

I FORGIVE YOU. I'M SORRY. THANK YOU. I LOVE YOU.

18.

_____

I FORGIVE YOU. I'M SORRY. THANK YOU. I LOVE YOU.

19.

_____

I FORGIVE YOU. I'M SORRY. THANK YOU. I LOVE YOU.

20.

_____

I FORGIVE YOU. I'M SORRY. THANK YOU. I LOVE YOU.

21.

_____

I FORGIVE YOU. I'M SORRY. THANK YOU. I LOVE YOU.

22.

_____

I FORGIVE YOU. I'M SORRY. THANK YOU. I LOVE YOU.

23.

_____

I FORGIVE YOU. I'M SORRY. THANK YOU. I LOVE YOU.

24.

_____

I FORGIVE YOU. I'M SORRY. THANK YOU. I LOVE YOU.

25.

_____

I FORGIVE YOU. I'M SORRY. THANK YOU. I LOVE YOU.

After going through the forgiveness process, how do you now feel? Report your feelings to prove to yourself the effect of this exercise. Don't worry if you initially end up feeling worse. We are detoxing negative energy that has been backed up in your system for *years*. Honor yourself! Be patient. Healing takes time. And most importantly, please don't forget to forgive yourself. You deserve relief, babe.

Notes:

Day Three

Feel Your Way To Money

Hello again, Beautiful!

Can I just tell you how proud I am of you for creating your forgiveness list and actually going through and forgiving everyone and everything that's been taking up precious space in your heart?

That alone deserves a delicious bubbly champagne toast. We ain't got time for resentment. We got money to manifest, baby!

I am betting $1,000 that you feel like a million bucks today after doing some serious clutter and crap clearing over the last 48 hours. The last 48 hours alone will cause major positive shifts to occur, but we still have 19 amazing days ahead of us!

Today I want to talk about your feelings. Yes, your feelings babe. Us women get so much slack for being overly emotional, touchy-feely creatures. If only the men knew that our feelings make us powerful manifestors.

Take that, #GirlPower!

Why are feelings important? How you feel about your future including everything you're manifesting is the biggest predeterminant of what your future will actually end up looking and feeling like.

Take a quick second to get in touch with your feelings and assess how you feel today. Happy? Stressed? Excited? Bitchy? Worried? Fearful? Joyful? Excited? Indifferent?

Human beings are unique creatures with a wide array of feelings. I like to see feelings as a way to gauge what we are manifesting. This isn't to say that if you come across stress, worry, and fear, that you will automatically manifest those feelings. However, stress, worry and fear are *telling* you something about your belief in manifesting something you want.

Creating more money in your life feels really good to you, doesn't it? The ironic thing here is that more money in itself isn't what's going to make you happy. It's the *feeling* of having more money that you are actually after.

Check in right now to see *why* you want more money. How would having an extra $1,000 in your bank account or wallet feel to you? Freeing? Joyful? Exciting? Fun? Liberating?

Close your eyes and visualize the $1,000 in your hand right now. Now that you have the money, what is it that you're going to do with it? It's important to note that it's what we *do* with the money that will bring us the feelings that we are after.

You know the quote, "money doesn't buy happiness?" Well, the quote exists because having a million dollars in the bank account alone will not bring you happiness. Money alone can't do anything.

Money alone makes us feel indifferent. Doing things with the money, the freedom it brings in our lives, the limitless possibilities *because* of the million dollars in the bank is what brings us happiness. Does that make sense?

We're always after the feelings of what money will bring us, not really the money itself. Money alone is just paper. It doesn't do anything sitting on its own. This is something to be aware of when manifesting money. Money is energy. In order to attract more money, you have to match its energy.

How exactly do we become an energetic match to the money? We get into the feeling as if we already have that extra $1,000 in our wallet, bank account, or wherever else we tend to keep our money.

It's also super crucial that we don't think of the money as if it's still coming, or not here yet. You really want to envision as if it's *already* here in your hand. Because it is! The manifestation has already taken place in the spiritual realm. It's up to you to bring it into the physical realm using your feelings of already having it.

Money Babe Action

So, what's today's money babe action?

List the 5 biggest feelings that the extra $1,000 in the next 21 days will bring into your life.

1.

2.

3.

4.

5.

Now, using the 5 feelings you just listed, actually physically feel those feelings right now. The more often you feel them, the more the universe conspires to bring you the actual physical things needed to keep feeling those feelings.

According to Law of Attraction, like attracts like. Feel the feelings to attract *more* of those feelings! Since money brings us those feelings, this is how we end up attracting the money. It's as simple as that!

Notes:

Day Four

The Massive Money Multiplier

Let's pretend you just put your heart and soul into buying or making someone a present that you just could not *wait* to give to them.

You spend all day shopping and all night putting it together, wrapping it in beautiful golden wrapping paper, and tying to it a beautiful puffy white bow. You even write a card that expresses how much you love them and how you hope they enjoy receiving the present as much as you enjoyed giving it.

Their birthday finally comes around, and you eagerly wait for them to open their gift. They unwrap your present, take a quick look at it, and toss it to the side, already moving on to the next present as if yours didn't even exist.

No acknowledgement. No thank you muttered. Not even any eye contact made. Nothing.

How would that make you feel? Pissed! Upset! Surprised! You'd never want to give them another gift again. Why even *bother* putting that much effort into another gift for such an unappreciative person?

If you have been waking up pissed off every morning, complaining about your coffee getting too cold too fast, how your children aren't as smart as you hoped they would be, and how your husband pays zero attention to you, and you have yet to see avalanches of abundance make their way into your bank account, then I have a perspective shift coming for you.

The same un-appreciation for life that you have is the sole reason why you have never experienced the miracles and magic of manifesting, let alone manifesting money. The Universe is the gift giver and you have yet to say thank you. Is it any surprise why gifts don't keep coming your way?

Did you wake up this morning and say "thank you" first thing? Are you grateful for each moment that passes you by? Do you appreciate every single thing that you have in your possession? If you answered no to the above questions, that's ok. It's not too late to make changes. You have your entire life ahead of you, and you are just getting started.

Gratitude is the holy grail of the high vibration energy that you can put out into the Universe. Whatever you are grateful for, you will see more of in your life. Whatever you take for granted, you will see less. It's literally up to you to choose how much good you want to see in your life based on the amount of gratitude you have for it.

God, the Universe, your Higher Power, whatever you believe in, is working overtime to bring you everything you've ever desired into your life. You are always being guided, protected, and taken care of.

Your heart is beating, you can see the words on this page, you are breathing just fine, and you are probably one of the few to be blessed with electricity, a roof over your head, warm, dry clothing, and a full belly.

There is so much to be grateful for already. There is so much to acknowledge the Universe for. If you don't yet have the kind of money you desire, it's not because you don't deserve it or you're incapable of earning it.

It's just that you haven't yet appreciated the money that you have already.

When you are grateful for what you have, you will always be given more. That's just how it works.

Today we are going to focus on gratitude by making a list of 25 things that you're grateful for. The list can include anything and everything that you can possibly be grateful for.

Finding things to be grateful for is so much easier than you think. Are you healthy? Can you walk? Talk? Breathe? Can you see? Do you have a job? A business that's supporting you? Did you drive a car today? Did you get to eat today? Are you wearing clothes? Is your heart beating? What else can you be grateful for?

Money Babe Action

1.

2.

3.

4.

5.

6.

7.

8.

_____

9.

_____

10.

_____

11.

_____

12.

_____

13.

_____

14.

_____

15.

_____

16.

_____

17.

_____

18.

_____

19.

_____

20.

_____

21.

_____

22.

_____

23.

_____

24.

_____

25.

_____

Make it a goal to create gratitude lists every single day. I have my clients tell me what they're most grateful for at the start of all of our sessions. The more high vibe appreciative energy we put out, the faster things come into our lives.

Gratitude is the key to open the channels to your divine abundance. It's time to start appreciating the Universe for all that it has given to you every single day without expecting a thing in return.

Notes:

```



```

Day Five

Giving Money A Purpose

Hello again, gorgeous! What are you grateful for today? Did you enjoy your list making yesterday? I bet you have realized that you truly have so much to be thankful for already. Life is already so sweet.

Today I want you to set the *intention* of manifesting your $1,000. Yes, I know, when you bought this book you obviously intended to manifest an extra thousand bucks into your life from the second you pushed the "buy" button. Duh. Why else would you have bought it?

However, I still want to go over intentions and share how you can use them to get really clear on what you want in your life.

You see, babe, money needs a purpose. It has no free will. It's just energy, remember? It is *you* who directs it to go where you want it to go. Unless it has a direction of where to flow, it'll just flow elsewhere.

You're planning on manifesting an extra thousand dollars into your life. Let's think about what you will be doing with this money. I want you to plan your life ahead as if this money is already in your hand, in your wallet, in your bank account, wherever it is easiest for you to visualize it.

For me, I like to visualize a balance in my bank account since I do all my finance related stuff online and hardly ever keep cash on me. Some people like to deal only with cash and it's easiest for them to visualize their wallets stuffed with cash. This part is totally dependent on your preferences.

Set an intention that no matter what, the $1,000 is already in your possession. It doesn't matter what your current reality says to you right now. It doesn't matter what bills you have to pay, what someone says to you, and what your bank balance is. The goal is to ignore your current reality and only visualize the reality that you want. This is a major #LifeHack tip.

You *already* have this extra $1,000 and you already have plans on how you're gonna spend it! Otherwise, you wouldn't desire it, right? Let's give your $1,000 an amazing purpose so that it can't help but come to you.

Today's money babe action is to make a list of what you will do with the money.

Direct it! Give it orders! Treat your list as a GPS for your money. You have to tell it where to go or it sits there aimlessly floating around, never really appearing into your reality.

Remember *you* are the master of money, not the other way around. Money is a neutral resource and what you do with it is *up to you*. It isn't good. It isn't evil. It is neutral. You give it the meaning that you want.

So, what will you do with your extra $1,000?

For example, your list can be something like :

1. Pay off the Citi Bank credit card: $200
2. Treat myself to a cut & color appointment with my favorite stylist: $240 with tip

3. Take my hard-working husband out to dinner to our fav restaurant: $50

4. Buy the table we really need for our living room: $350

5. Upgrade our groceries to all organic this week because of our new health goals: $60 on top of regular bill

6. Donate $100 to my favorite charity

Total: $1,000

When you intend to have this money, show the Universe exactly what you'll do with it, feel the feelings of having it, amazing shifts start to happen. Even if you plan on saving some of it, that's totally ok too. But remember: give it the *direction* to be put into a savings account. Let's get specific here.

The Universe conspires on a full-time basis to make your nonphysical intentions become a physical reality. It's literally like placing an order in a cosmic catalog. Place your order, receive your order. That's the beauty of manifesting.

I personally love to relate manifesting to ordering something on Amazon. It helps me put my trust into the process and prevents me from overcomplicating it.

To place an order for what I want, I log onto Amazon.com. I find what I want. I put it in my shopping cart. I place my order. Amazon receives it. They deliver my package. I don't get attached to the guys at Amazon asking them where my package is 100 times a day. I don't stress about getting something different than what I ordered. I know it is on its way as soon as I place my order. I trust Amazon to deliver it, and the package always comes exactly as ordered 9.9 times out of 10. The last 0.1 is left to any delays that may occur, just like we sometimes have what we want delayed by the Universe to ensure it manifests in a way that's for our highest good. Delays aren't denials. You ordered your package, so you're getting it.

You may be thinking, *yeah right, like it's actually this simple.* Well, it is, but I did forget to mention something.

The money won't magically appear in your lap out of thin air. That's just not how physics works. Manifesting doesn't defy physics. There is action involved. You are half of the co-creating equation while the Universe is the other half. The action is super easy. It doesn't even feel like action. It doesn't even feel like hard work. It's just like pushing the order button on Amazon. I'll explain more on this later on in the book.

All you need to do right now is to direct your money and intend for it to appear. *That's it.*

Money Babe Action

1. What will you do with your $1,000? How will you spend it?

_____

_____

_____

2. How is it going to feel spending, saving, and investing it?

_____

_____

_____

3. How will an extra $1,000 in 21 days support you and enhance your life?

_____

_____

_____

4. How does it feel now knowing that you are giving money a purpose and it has no other choice but to appear in your life to support you?

_____

_____

_____

5. Have you been giving money a purpose before? If not, why?

_____

_____

_____

6. Rewrite this statement and release it to the Universe: I am in the process of manifesting $1,000. I trust that the $1,000 is on its way to me right now and will appear by the 21st day. And it is so, for the highest good of all involved.

Notes:

Day Six

The "How" Is Not Your Job

Are you starting to feel anxious about how exactly the money is going to come? If you are, you're not alone. I know you're feeling this way because everyone new to manifesting money shares this same feeling. *How the hell is this extra $1,000 going to appear when I have a job with a fixed income? When my business isn't growing? When I already have all these bills to pay? How, Kathrin, how?*

Here's the thing. You'll never actually know how. I don't know how, you don't know how, no one knows how, but that's the least of your worries. The biggest lesson I learned in my own manifesting journey was to completely detach myself from the "how."

Money comes in the most *unexpected* ways. Using this exact 21-day challenge, I set a goal to manifest an extra $2k in a 21-day period. I was very new to manifesting money. Like you, I had zero clue how it was going to happen.

I began to learn really quickly that the "how" is never up to you. It is not your job, it is not your worry, it is not your responsibility. Your only job is to release yourself from all the details, and just focus on the destination.

The unexpectedness of manifesting is why this process is so much fun.

That's the point. It's *fun*. It's a game you play! It's those moments of *Holy shit, is this happening? Did I just manifest this?* that make it even more epic. It's not supposed to be stressful.

So how did I end up manifesting the $2k using this exact process as a complete newbie to manifesting money?

My $2,000 came from my mom (who didn't pay my bills at the time, didn't even know my credit card login) when she somehow made a $1,000 payment on my credit card 1 week after I set the intention of putting $1,000 of the manifested money onto the credit card. Funny how that worked out, isn't it?

And the other $1,000?

I initially owed on my taxes that year because I was a business owner in a network marketing/direct sales company. *Something* told me to wait until the very last day to pay my taxes. My mom (again, my guardian angel sent by the Universe) called me one random day to tell me that a woman at her work wants to help me file for a tax return. I thought it was interesting and gladly gave up my paperwork to her. The very next day, I got a text that I was getting a $1,000 refund.

My $2,000 manifested. Just like that. In a completely unexpected way. Was there any way I could have predicted my money manifesting this way? There was no way in hell.

Remember: the "how" isn't up to you. Detach, detach, detach. All you have to do is ask for the money, feel the feelings of the money already being here, intend for it to manifest, and let go.

Stop thinking about it. The more you stress and worry about it, the more you are showing the Universe that you don't trust in the process. That energy of distrust ends up manifesting more distrust, thus no money coming your way. It's a cycle.

Today's money babe action is simple. Distract yourself in a way that serves you and makes you happy. Let go of any thoughts that don't serve you.

Money Babe Action

Answer the questions and pick something fun to do today.

1. What can you do today to amplify the feelings of already having the money while you detach yourself from "how" it's going to happen?

_____

_____

_____

_____

2. What are 5 things that make you happy when you spend time doing them?

3. Which one stands out the most to you right now?

Do that thing today. Whether it's to get a massage, call up a friend for some catching up, go to a wine tasting, or take a spin class, what you end up doing doesn't matter.

Things happen faster when you're having fun!

Day Seven

Negativity Detox

Be positive, be positive, be positive!

How many times were you told to *just be positive* in the countless self-help books you have encountered over the years?

In a world like the one we live in today, it's easy to roll our eyes at the thought of staying positive.

Facebook friends complaining. Fox news telling us that the world is coming to an end. Coworkers reminding us how underpaid and broke we all are. Business owners letting us know that most businesses fail in their first year. Friends draining us with their problems asking us to fix them. Newspapers making sure we are aware the economy is crashing--again.

I will be the last person to bullshit you into thinking that you can be happy, cheerful, and positive 100% of the time. However, that doesn't mean to give up and give in. We're human beings and we were built to experience many more emotions than just the positive ones. We experience negative emotions and negative circumstances because there is an important lesson that we have yet to learn behind them, and must learn it in order to evolve.

If everything was always perfect, how would we grow? How would we learn? How would we advance to the next level? We just wouldn't. And so, life throws us the occasional curve ball.

Remember when I said you are always divinely protected, guided and loved? I mean it. No matter what happens in your life, it is always for your highest good and advantage. It's happening for a reason because it's serving a purpose. It's for you to experience in order to grow.

Yet, even so, we can choose to be intentional with the information that we allow into our precious heads. Just because we can't always be in control of everything, doesn't mean we need to give up and immerse ourselves in everyone's pity party--including our own. Protecting your mindset and being intentional with what you choose to focus on will help you keep your vibration high and help you stay focused on attracting all the amazing things you want into your life --like money.

My goal today is to encourage you to take some time off from all the negativity that isn't serving you. Find the sources of negativity that you *can* control and stop paying attention to them. Stop focusing on them.

This can be done by:

- Unfollowing people who do nothing but complain on social media and share negative news

- Turning off the news and going on a news fast

- Spending less and less time hanging out with friends who do nothing but gossip about others and complain about everything

- Changing the subject when family members or coworkers start to complain about money or focus on scarcity

Tuning into negativity that we *do* have control over affects us more than we're willing to admit or even notice. Personally, I haven't watched the news in over 15 years. I purposefully tune out any fear-based messaging that I know will have a negative effect on my mindset. I am extremely protective of what I tune into because I know what an impact it has on my ability to manifest freely and easily.

We can't control everything in our lives, but we can be intentional with most of it.

Today's money babe action is to go on a negativity cleanse. Unfollow the people you know you need to unfollow. Spend less time with the people you know you need to spend less time with. Stop visiting the websites that do not make you feel empowered, positive, and joyful. Think before you turn on your go-to news station. Toss the newspaper before you even open it.

Because our minds work like vacuums, and will crave being filled up with something else, today's money babe action is to *also* go on a positivity binge. Find successful, happy, and fulfilled people who inspire you and see what they're up to. Hang with them. Pick up on some of their habits. Try meditating at a local yoga and meditation studio. Find a podcast in the self-help section of iTunes and tune into a couple of episodes. Watch inspiring Ted Talks on YouTube. Pick up another new book in the self-help section of Barnes & Noble.

Intentionally go out of your way to prove to yourself that the world is a much more beautiful, inspiring, and positive place than we give it credit for. You will always end up finding what you're looking for, so look for what you want to see in the world.

The goal here is to start shaping your reality into one that serves you. You have an energy field around you that works like a magnet. When choosing to focus on negativity, you will end up attracting negative people, situations, and circumstances. When choosing to focus on positivity, you will end up attracting positive people, situations, and circumstances.

It's universal law and it doesn't work any other way.

Money Babe Action

1. List all the sources of negativity that you have been tuning into.

2. What are you committed to giving up that isn't serving you?

3. List all the new sources of positivity that you can tune into instead.

4. What are you committed to tuning into that will allow you to grow into the most positive version of yourself?

_____

_____

_____

Notes:

[ ]

Day 8

Creating Money

As a kid, do you remember how excited you were to go on treasure hunts? You were given a map with a bunch of clues and your only goal that day was to find the hidden treasure. The incredible gold at X marks the spot.

You would spend *all day* looking for that damn treasure, and it kept you busy for hours. There was so much excitement in knowing that at any point in time you were just *feet* from the gold. Finding the so-called "gold" felt pretty much like the kid equivalent to finding a million dollars and boy, were you determined.

Today we're going to replicate that excitement by going on a treasure hunt for money. Yes, an adult treasure hunt. Except the gold we are looking for this time, are pennies, dimes, nickels, quarters, and dollar bills. Any amount that you find today is considered gold.

Today's main focus is on finding money. Anywhere, everywhere, wherever. It can be behind the couch, in the corner of your kitchen, on the street, hidden in your pockets, between the seat and the console of your car, a random drawer, etc.

Whatever you will look for, you will usually find. What you focus on, expands. Start seeing the world as an abundant place, and you will start to notice pennies on the ground, maybe even a quarter or a ten-dollar bill.

The biggest mistake I see people make is to see a penny on the ground and walk right by it. Or even worse, kick it to the side. It's just a penny, why bother? It's not *really* money, is it? However, money is money is money.

Wealthy, abundant people understand this. If you're "too good" to pick up a penny off the ground and celebrate it like you just found $100, then you're "too good" for any money at all! If you can't respect a penny, you can't be trusted with $1,000.

Any bit of gold you pick up, is still gold. Celebrate every single bit of money you find as if you just picked up your $1,000. The Universe and your subconscious mind don't know the difference between real or imagined. If you actually found $1,000 on the ground or just imagined it, the result is the exact same.

You will attract more of the same feelings, which attracts more money. Acting "as if" is a really powerful trick in manifesting. How would you feel if you found money on the ground? Pretty excited, right?

Part one of today's money babe action is to look around for money. Look for pennies, nickels, dimes, and so on. Celebrate the fact that the Universe is abundant. Look for your treasure, you big kid!

Say to yourself over and over again as an affirmation: "Money is all around me. I find money everywhere. It flows effortlessly into my life on a daily basis."

With each penny you find, show gratitude towards it. Remember the lesson on gratitude? What we are thankful for, show gratitude toward, and focus on, expands. It's not bullshit. It is *law*.

Make a note of all the money you find all around you. Keep a log so that you can keep track and physically see the proof of money expanding and multiplying right before your very eyes.

Part two of today's money babe action is to do a little bit of brainstorming.

I want to help you get your creative juices flowing and open up the channels of how the money is going to come into your life. I like to focus on creating money rather than earning it. When you think of earning more money, resistance tends to build up because who wants to work more? Instead, when you think of money as creating more of it, the resistance tends to fall off and it shows up in our lives through the paths of least resistance.

Money Babe Action

Write a list of 10 ways you can make or create more money in your life *today*.

To give you an example, here is a list I whipped up real quick

1. Sell my old paintings that everyone has been telling me to put up for auction.

2. Offer my neighbors to babysit their twins while they go on a date night this Friday.

3. Finally ask my boss for that raise I've been thinking about for the last 6 months

4. Sign up a new client or up-sell an existing client to a higher-end package

We're working on expanding your thinking and shifting your perspective. So many women get stuck wondering how in the world more money can come to them. Even though the Universe is in charge of the "how," it helps us get into "receiving mode" faster when we get our own creative juices flowing and take massive action.

This is one of the best ways to reduce resistance to money. Feel free to start your money flow process by actually taking action on some of the things on your list!

Now, it's your turn:

1.

_____

2.

_____

3.

_____

4.

_____

5.

_____

6.

_____

7.

_____

8.

_____

9.

_____

10.

_____

P.S. How much money did you end up finding today? Use the next page to track every single penny, dime, nickel, quarter, and dollar bill you find today.

Day Nine

Affirming Your Money Truths

Hey again gorgeous soul!

Did you find lots of money yesterday? How did finding unexpected money make you feel?

I bet by now you're noticing that money is truly abundant and it appears into your life in the most incredible, expected and *unexpected* ways.

Remember the affirmation I gave you yesterday for finding money? If you don't, it was: *"Money is all around me. I find money everywhere. It flows effortlessly into my life on a daily basis."*

Chant this all day, every day.

Today I want to give you many more money affirmations. The reason why I am such a big fan of affirmations is because they are extremely useful in training your subconscious brain.

Just like each limiting belief around money started as a single thought that repeated itself over and over again until it was absorbed by your subconscious like a sponge and manifested into money struggle, we have to work our affirmations in a similar fashion.

Affirmations are used by stating a positive phrase that represents what it is that you want to manifest. It's highly recommended to back up each of the affirmations with as much emotion as possible. You want to *feel* them as absolute truth. Without this emotion, it sounds like any other statement that you could be saying to yourself.

Saying them the first few times is kinda weird. Not gonna lie here. But after a while, saying them out loud to yourself enough times, your subconscious mind begins to absorb them and you start to feel as if it is already your current reality.

You are just speaking your new truth out loud and watching the Universe manifest each affirmation before your eyes.

For today's money babe action, choose 3 affirmations that resonate with you most out of the options I give below.

Repeat them out loud to yourself as many times as needed until you feel the truth behind each one. I like to do my affirmations in the car where I know no one will hear me, or standing in wonder woman pose first thing in the morning as part of my morning ritual.

Feel free to make up a few of your own that feel really good to you.

The Affirmations

1. Money comes my way quickly and easily.
2. People love to give me money/pay me.
3. I deserve to be highly paid for the work that I do.
4. I am worthy of all the money that I receive.

5. I love money. Money loves me.

6. Money is attracted to me and finds its way into my life quickly and easily.

7. I create new money making opportunities on a daily basis.

8. I am a magnet for money. Prosperity is drawn to me.

9. Money comes to me in expected and unexpected ways.

10. I am so worthy of making more money.

11. I am open and ready to receive all the wealth life offers me.

12. I release all negative energy that I have tied to money.

13. I use money to better my life and the lives of others.

14. Wealth constantly flows into my life.

15. My actions create constant prosperity.

16. I am aligned with the energy of abundance.

17. My finances are improving at a rate beyond my wildest dreams.

18. Money is the root of joy and comfort.

19. Money and spirituality can co-exist in harmony.

20. I am at peace with having a lot of money.

21. I can handle massive success with grace.

22. Money expands my life's opportunities and experiences.

Sometimes, some of these affirmations feel like total and complete bullshit.

This is normal. Especially when we are just starting out and opening ourselves to positive self-talk.

Something that helped me when I first started was to add "I am choosing to believe…" or "I am in the process of believing that…" before each affirmation. My clients, the ones that were very new to manifesting and built up some resistance, loved these additions.

These stepping stone affirmation additions will help you believe your affirmations faster than trying to push through any resistance you encounter.

Keep in mind that affirmations are like working out and eating right when embarking on a weight loss journey. You won't see results overnight, but over time the slight seemingly invisible changes compound to make a *huge* difference.

If you want to take your affirmation practice a step further, there are countless apps available that you can download and have affirmations pop up on your phone all day long. I probably have 15 programmed into my phone and it's made a huge difference in my life. These have become my favorite phone notifications!

With certain apps, you can either choose to set a time for a specific affirmation to go off, or have them appear randomly in divine timing. If you don't find an app that you like, feel free to utilize the old-fashioned alarm system. Create alarms to go off on your phone throughout the day and name them with whichever affirmations you choose. Super easy to set up.

Money Babe Action

1. What are the 3 affirmations you chose to commit to and affirm your money truth with?

2. How do you feel the first time saying each of these statements?

3. Spend the entire day repeating these three affirmations. Remember to back them up with a lot of emotion. How did you feel about them by the end of the day?

_____

_____

_____

If you're still having a hard time believing them, try standing in a wonder woman pose for 60 seconds before saying them again. You'll feel a physical shift happening in your body that will allow your confidence levels to shoot up and accept what you're saying as truth.

4. Did you program any affirmations into your phone? If so, which ones did you program to go off and when?

_____

_____

_____

Day Ten

Shut Your Mind Up

Let me fill you in on a little secret, babe. My *best* money making ideas and opportunities came to me when I completely silenced my mind.

What do I mean by silencing my mind? Yep, you guessed it. I'm talking about meditation.

I don't know about you, but my mind normally races at a thousand miles per hour. I have thoughts and ideas coming at me so often, and so fast, it's not uncommon for me to lay awake at 3 am strategizing how the hell I'm ever going to fall asleep. Trust me, I've already tried journaling, writing them down, and any other strategies to release them, but the crazy continues. And so one day I turned to meditation.

Like me, you may have initially laughed at the concept of meditation. Why sit still for such a long time when you can use that time to be so much more productive? As a chronic hyper-achiever who thrived off of productivity, meditation looked like a major joke. *What the hell was it even for? How do you just sit there for hours?!*

That was until I tried it. I decided to give in, turned on a random guided meditation I found on the internet, and for the first time in my life I started to think clearly again. The voices calmed down, and clarity hit me like a ton of bricks.

I soon became obsessed with it and couldn't live without it. Especially when the money-making ideas started to peacefully, and calmly appear as a result of sitting still and just opening myself up to *listening*. It became my daily practice.

Incredible money making ideas come when you're still, listening, and ready to receive. You spend so much time asking for guidance, asking for money to show up, but how much time do you spend listening to your instructions?

Trust me on this. When you shut your mind up, your subconscious mind speaks. Your subconscious mind is the magic place that holds *all* your money receiving answers coming straight from the limitless Universal intelligence.

Sometimes the guidance from Universal intelligence doesn't even make its way to you *during* the meditation. Most of the time it comes right after. I have had many light bulb moments go off for me while I was in the shower.

It made me realize quickly that meditation isn't necessarily the action. It's the *beginning* of the action. It's the signal you send to the Universe letting it know that your mind is clear and you are ready to listen. You have set the intention to receive your guidance, and so it comes. It could even be while you're on the toilet. The Universe doesn't discriminate on the perfect moment.

In the beginning, you may find that guided meditations work best for you.

As you grow through your practice, you may graduate to complete stillness and silence. The secret to meditation is to do what works for you. I used to meditate by laying in bed with my eyes closed. Now, I practice mudras (those special hand positions you see Yogis make while meditating) and I like to sit up straight. It doesn't matter what works for you as long as it *works*. Make it easy on yourself.

Your money babe action for today? You guessed it. *Meditation.* There are thousands of guided meditations that you can try on the internet. In fact, there are apps aimed at newbie meditators with guided meditations that are only 10 minutes long. We all have 10 minutes to spare in our day.

Your money babe action is to meditate for at least 10 minutes. Yep, that's it. Choose what speaks to you and give it a try. You can't do it wrong. I promise.

Money Babe Action

After the meditation, answer the following questions:

1. How I felt before the meditation:

_____

_____

_____

2. My stress/anxiety/worry level on a scale of 1-10 pre-meditation:

_____

_____

3. The meditation practice that I chose today:

_____

_____

4. How I felt during the meditation:

_____

_____

_____

5. How I felt right after:

_____

_____

_____

6. My stress/anxiety/worry level on a scale of 1-10 post meditation:

_____

_____

7. Ideas/Thoughts, if any, that appeared in my mind once I silenced it:

_____

8. Brilliant money making ideas, if any, that popped into my head during the meditation.

9. Brilliant money making ideas, if any, that popped into my head later in the day:

Notes:

Day Eleven

You Must See It Before You See It

Have you ever thought of a friend and just minutes later, that friend called you? Started to crave a certain food, and "coincidentally" your spouse asked you if you wanted to go out and grab some of exactly what you were craving? Or maybe you had the experience of someone saying something the second you started thinking it?

These are just some of the interesting coincidences we have most likely experienced in our day-to-day lives. However, here's the truth about coincidences. There is no such thing, babe.

Everything you can imagine, think of, or visualize, has the potential to actualize into your physical reality. These were just experiences you had manifesting on the spot. You visualized something, and it appeared instantly in your reality.

As a child, how often were you caught staring outside the window of your classroom instead of at the chalkboard in front of you? Children are really good at visualizing, and unfortunately we are taught that visualizing, or daydreaming, was a bad thing. We were scolded for not paying attention in class, and slowly lost a powerful manifesting skill. We slowly got less and less visually creative as we grew up.

We stopped daydreaming. And daydreaming is the key to an exciting, fulfilling, incredible future. Interesting how that happened. Today you have my full permission to start daydreaming again. Daydream to your heart's desire. See everything that you could ever want to live out in your mind. See the $1,000 manifesting over and over again.

This kind of daydreaming is called visualization. Visualization is one of the fastest ways to bring your manifestations into fruition. This is because most of everything in the entire Universe started as just a single idea that came into someone's mind.

Think about it. The iPhone, iPad, or MacBook and other incredible technology we sometimes take for granted? Started in Steve Job's imagination long before they ended up in your hands.

Wherever you go in your mind, you *will* experience it in your body. Olympic athletes do this all the time. They visualize themselves running their race long before their feet ever step onto the tracks. It's part of their training. It's part of their winning strategy. Olympic athletes are known to hire top-notch mindset coaches to keep their mindsets in check the entire time they're training for their events. It's not just about how their body performs, but also how they *envision* their bodies performing. This shit isn't made up. It's science.

So, how do we visualize? Really simple. Let's do a visualization exercise based on the $1,000 that you are manifesting into your life right now.

Close your eyes and see your hands raised out in front of you with a stack of hundreds in your palms.

- How does it look?
- How does it smell?
- What does it feel like?

- Why does it feel so good?

- What are you wearing in this moment?

- Who are you sharing the good news with about your new monetary addition?

- What do you see doing with the money?

- Are you hearing any music in the background?

- What's the weather like while you hold onto this money?

- Is it sunny? Windy? Warm? Cold?

- Are you in your house?

- Or are you at a bank?

Visualization is all about *details*. It's about being as clear as you can possibly get. Don't freak out if you are having trouble with this at first. As someone with very strong visualization skills, this is a really easy process for me. However, for some of you, it might be more challenging. If you can't exactly see things around you, then just focus on the feelings. Someone just gave you $1,000 cash. *How do you feel right now?*

Remember the lesson about the "how?" Don't forget that super important lesson. Your goal right now is to not even think about the "how did I even get this cash in the first place?" All that matters right now is the end product. You are already holding the cash. Keep your focus in the "it's already happened" zone.

Feel the abundance. Feel the joy. Feel the happiness. Go back to those feelings that you wrote down earlier in the book that this money will bring you. Those are the feelings that will help you manifest.

Remember, it is not the *thoughts* necessarily that end up manifesting, but more so the *feelings*. If we manifested every thought we've ever had, well, we'd be in trouble! Therefore, the Universe responds to the vibration of your *feelings* which is a result of a thought on repeat.

I like to spend about 10 minutes a day visualizing. I put on an upbeat song, crank up the volume, put in my headphones, lie down, and see myself doing the exact things that I want to manifest.

I visualize being in the places I want to manifest. Hearing the good news that I want to manifest. I smile, I laugh, I cry. I go full out because I know in order for me to go to these places and do these things in the body, I must first see it all with my mind.

Another really great tool for visualizing is to create a kickass vision board. Vision boards are basically a collection of pictures and words that represent what you want to manifest. Creating vision boards can be *really* fun because it gives you a visual destination for your metaphorical life GPS.

I create a new vision board about every 6 months as I manifest things and as my desires change. Vision boards can also be used in the visualization process that I described earlier as a tool to actually help you see what it is that you want to be focusing on. I made a video for you on *How To Create A Vision Board That Actually Manifests* and you can find it in my freebie library at ManifestationBabe.com

Watch it and create one!

Money Babe Action

Your money babe action today is fun and simple.

Either spend 10 minutes visualizing the $1,000 in your hand, or create a vision board filled with pictures that represent everything you will be doing once you have that money. Go wild here!

When you are done, come back and answer these questions:

1. What did you envision?

2. How did it look to you?

3. What did it smell like?

_____

_____

4. How did you feel holding this much money in your hands knowing it's all yours?

_____

_____

5. Who were you with?

_____

_____

_____

6. What were you saying to yourself?

_____

_____

_____

7. Where were you?

_____

_____

8. What did you spend the money on?

_____

_____

_____

9. What did you hear around you?

_____

_____

_____

10. Can you repeat this exercise holding even more money or envisioning something else that you want to manifest?

_____

_____

_____

_____

Notes:

Day Twelve

Your Word Is Your Wand

Growing up, how often did your mother tell you to watch your language or you will have some sort of privilege taken away from you? For me, it was *always* my precious cell phone.

Today, I'm going to bring you back to those days when you were not allowed to say bad words or you would get punished. Today is the day you learn to *watch your language* as it pertains to money.

What do I mean here? Well, if the child version of this was to have your cell phone taken away, the adult equivalent is having money taken away from you.

We certainly don't want *that*, right?!

Allow me to explain.

How many times have you said the following phrases?

"I can't afford _____."

"That's too expensive."

"I wish I could buy _____."

"Maybe when I'm rich I'll do _____"

"Those rich people _____."

"That's for rich people."

"Sorry, I can't. I'm broke right now."

Did you know that whenever you say these phrases you are literally creating affirmations that perpetuate a scarcity mentality? You are manifesting everything that you declare out loud to the world whether you are consciously aware of it or not.

When you say you can't afford something, you're manifesting the fact that you'll never afford it. When you say that something is expensive, guess what? It will *always* be expensive! If something is for "rich people" and you don't see yourself as rich, then you'll never have this desire that is apparently only saved for "rich people."

Even if what you're saying is *technically* true, like for instance, you literally can't buy something that has a price tag of $1,000 that you really want, pretend like you can! Act as if. I don't mean to go $1,000 in debt. What I mean is to pretend that you have the $1,000 sitting in your bank account right now and actually buy it using your imagination. Visualize yourself spending the money and acquiring the thing just as if it were actually happening. Feel all the feelings you would actually feel if this thing was in your possession.

You may not be physically spending the money, but energetically, you totally are. I do mental energetic spending all the time as one of my money manifesting tricks. I walk around a store, the mall, or even a street of beautiful houses I want, and just "buy" things. Mentally spending the money all day long. I constantly repeat to myself, "Wow, so cheap! I can afford this. I can afford that. Thank you!"

So instead of perpetuating a reality of being broke forever, you can start saying to yourself instead:

"I CAN afford _____."

"I love being so rich and so wealthy that I can do ___."

"I have SO much money flowing into my bank account right now. It's so exciting."

"Wow, everything is so cheap!"

I don't care what your circumstances are telling you right now because at an energetic level everything you ever desired is already yours. It's a matter of matching your vibration to the vibration of the object/event/situation that you desire in order to bring it into the physical realm.

You create your reality every second of the day. You are always co-creating with your creator, and you have all the power to decide what it is that you want. Whatever you want, you can have. Speak it into existence on a daily basis. The $1,000 you're trying to manifest from the daily lessons in this book? It's already in your wallet, pocket, bank account. Remember this.

Enough of the self-sabotaging, self-limiting phrases. Your words have insane power over your life. As Frances Scovel Shinn titles one of her books, your word is your *wand*. Only speak what you want to come true.

Money Babe Action

Your money babe action today is to start speaking only what you want to manifest and answer the following questions.

1. What are some of the limiting phrases you have been saying lately that are related to money?

_____

_____

_____

2. Where did they come from? Who did you learn them from?

_____

_____

_____

3. Can you see how they've been manifesting into your reality? Can you find examples of you literally living out what you are saying?

4. Can you replace these limiting phrases with their opposite counterpart?

5. Which phrases are you committed to saying from now on to create the reality that you *do* want?

Day Thirteen

Your Gut Is Talking. Listen Up.

By now, you're probably thinking: Okay, Kathrin. This is all fun and stuff, but do I wait for money to fall into my lap? Or do I have to go out and get this money? I always hear that taking action is important. Do I have to take action when manifesting money?

Yes. And no. The idea and goal of manifesting with ease is not to take just *any* action. The goal is to listen closely and take *inspired* action.

Because you are a co-creator of your reality, you are one half of the equation when it comes to manifesting the money you desire. This means that there is work involved on your end. But the work? It's actually *really* easy and doesn't even feel like work at all.

Allow me to explain.

As you increase your money vibe during the 21-day journey, you might notice your intuition starting to speak to you. Maybe even for the first time ever. You are receiving little nudges here and there nudging you to do certain things, think a certain way, or to see something new you've never noticed before.

Maybe you are being nudged to call someone, to take a different route to work, or go to a different cafe for your usual breakfast choice of an almond milk latte and protein bar. These nudges feel automatic and come into your mind for no apparent reason. They feel really easy.

Your intuition is the thing that's going to help you manifest $1,000 because it's the deep part of you that's regularly communicating with the Universe. So, as you increase your money vibe, act as if you already have the money, visualize it, and do the daily assignments, you will receive more and more inspiration to do certain things. It will all feel really natural and seem as if you made it all up yourself. Like you had a thought pop up, and acting on it was the obvious next thing to do. Hence, the inspired action.

Remember my own experience of manifesting $2,000 for the first time following this exact 21-day process? *Something* told me to wait until the very last day to file my taxes that year. That something was *my* inspired action. That *something* inspired my *mom* to make a $1,000 payment on one of my credit cards! Yes, our inspired action can come through and inspire other people as well.

I've been *inspired* before to check for airline tickets at a time I wouldn't normally look at them just to notice that a flight I've been eyeing for a while randomly dropped in price, saving me $400 and getting the ticket at the exact price I wanted.

I've been inspired before to take a different route to a place I usually go to just to find my friend in there who sees me and ends up asking me if I can coach them in exchange for pay. Thus, manifesting money (and a new client) that I intended to bring into my life earlier that week.

How in the world could I ever have predicted these events? I simply couldn't have. It was up to my intuition to guide me into taking my inspired action. All the money channels open when you're willing to shut up and listen to your gut. Your gut is talking to you all the time.

Are you listening?

Your $,1000 will most likely come through your own inspired action. Be open to the nudges you receive over the next couple of days. Listen very carefully, listen very closely and have faith that the money is already yours. You're just waiting on the instructions to open up the channel.

You may have even noticed that your intuition has already been nudging you to do things or start something. Maybe it's to start a business? Write a book? Create your own course based on something you're super passionate about? Sell some things around the house? Hold a garage sale? I mean, the options here are endless.

Trust yourself to follow what you're being told to do. It's all very intuitive, but when you know, you know. It just feels so right, so pay attention to the feelings you're having about the actions.

It's so important to remember that your money can come to you in the most *unexpected* way. When most of my students and clients are asked if they expected their $1,000 to come in the ways that it actually came in, 99.9% will agree that the Universe surprised them with a much better route, plan, and outcome.

Money Babe Action

Today's money babe action is to get quiet, listen, and pay attention to your gut. Feel free to meditate to silence your mind and open your intuition to flow freely. Here are some questions to guide you:

1. Have you been noticing any nudges lately?

_____

_____

_____

_____

2. What has your gut been telling you?

3. Do you have an idea of how your $1,000 may come through to you?

4. How does it feel to take action on what your gut is telling you?

5. Does it feel scary? Empowering? Natural?

_____

_____

6. What do you believe your next step to take is? What feels like your inspired action to you?

_____

_____

_____

If you do not yet know, come back to these questions in a few days when you've received your first nudge from the Universe.

Notes:

Day Fourteen

Owning Your Shit

Sometime in early 2016 I found myself in over $25,000 of debt. As most people would, I stuck my head in the sand when it came to my finances. I didn't want to know what was in my bank account, and how much I owed on my credit cards.

Debt scared the crap out of me, but so did money.

For several months, I ignored looking at the exact number in my bank account or on my credit card statements. I just knew the approximate number, squinted my eyes when opening up statements, and made sure to look at the minimum payment due so I wouldn't miss it.

I never knew when automatic withdrawals would come out of my bank account. Any memberships I had ongoing like apps on my phone, gym memberships, music subscriptions like Spotify, etc. would come out of my bank account and I would just *hope* that the money would be there to cover it.

Budgeting weekly expenses for me was scary, an annoyance, and a huge frustration. If that wasn't enough, I overdrew my bank account at least once a week. Sometimes even twice. Those pesky letters that banks used to send out for every single overdraw letting you know about the mishap? That was like the *only* mail I would receive.

Sound like a familiar experience to you? Maybe you're going through this right now and are digging your head in the same sand that I was.

Finally owning up to my money was a major money shift for me. After so many years of struggle, it was time to own my shit. My gut was telling me that I had to face it in order to do something about it.

I didn't realize how much straight up *neglecting* my finances was affecting my money game. I didn't like to spend time with my money, and so it was no wonder money didn't like to spend time with me. *That was a powerful realization for me.* I was irresponsible. I showed my money no love. No respect. I didn't even acknowledge it when it did come around!

Babe, this is something that I want you to realize. You and your money are in a relationship. In many ways, this relationship is one of the most important ones you'll ever have in your life.

Money is often the reason for divorce, and the reason for misery among families. When money is hard to come by, there's nothing else to do but stress and worry about money from morning to night. Where is the fun in that?

I want you to look at your money as an extremely important relationship between you and your finances. If you neglect your husband, boyfriend, partner, or any of your friends, do you think the relationships will succeed? I bet you're shaking your head right now because it's a big fat NO.

I don't have to be a psychic to predict that whatever your relationship is with your finances right now, is exactly what's reflected in your bank account. Your relationship with money also determines how easily it manifests in your life. Manifesting money is really *easy* and *effortless* but we block that easy and effortless flow. We make money hard for ourselves by complicating our relationship with it. Boo.

However, I have really great news for you. We can make a choice right now to own up to our neglect and rebuild our relationship with the dollar bill.

Your money babe action today is a big one, and an oh so important one.

It's time to open every single credit card statement, bank account, and wallet you have cash in, and assess how much money you have and where it is going. Track when you receive income or get paid.

Figure out when your expenses come out of your accounts like when you pay your mortgage, rent, childcare, groceries, etc. Track down as much as you can. You want to know the dates, the amounts, and all the details in between.

This also includes looking at your debt if you're in debt. Yeah. I know. Scary shit. But so worth it. Being a teacher of the Law of Attraction, I initially feared that owning my debt would put me into the vibration of being debt, thus attracting more of it into my life. However, as my money manifesting journey progressed, I learned that taking ownership of your finances means you are someone who takes care of money. Money wants someone to take care of it. Money likes responsible people. Seeing how much you owe is being responsible.

Debt is not a bad thing. You are not a bad person for having debt or not having a clear idea of where your money is going. I want to make that super clear. People get into the vibration of guilt and shame when it comes to money, and my goal is not to shame you here or make you feel guilty of your past spending history. It's quite the opposite actually.

Just as your spouse, child, mother and best friend expect you to be honest with them, respect them, and prioritize your relationship with them, money is going to appreciate the same thing.

There is not guilt or shame involved here. The choices you have made are now in your past. We are letting go and creating a new compelling, exciting, and financially free future. Which starts with manifesting $1,000!

Just like anything else in this Universe, what you focus on expands. What you track, increases. What you are grateful for, flourishes and multiplies. The same goes with money. Repeat that to yourself as you own up to your money relationship.

Say it with me: What I focus on, expands. What I track, increases. What I'm grateful for, flourishes. Focus on your money, track your money, be grateful for every penny, and watch it grow.

One thing you can get into the practice of as of today is to check your bank account *DAILY*. Yes, every single day. Something that really helped me turn this into an exciting, uplifting, positive experience was to put on a high vibe upbeat song, make a fancy drink, and light a candle when checking my accounts. The point is to make the process enjoyable so that you can neuro-associate money with having fun. And remember, no matter what the amount is in there, **BE GRATEFUL FOR IT.**

I still remember the days when I would open my account and see numbers in the red. However, I still remained grateful. How did I do that? I noticed all the things that I had in my surroundings. I had a roof over my head, I had breakfast in front of me, and I was healthy. I found things to be grateful for no matter what was in my account. I also decided to start showing gratitude for any bills that I received. Whenever I received a bill for anything, I would show gratitude for the services that the bill has brought me. Whether it was gratitude for my apartment when seeing my rent bill, or gratitude for the fact that I had another month of Wi-Fi to enjoy the internet thanks to my electricity bill, I would make sure to show it.

Paying a bill is just an energetic exchange for a service rendered that you got to enjoy without doing any work on your end. Did you actually build your apartment building? Your house? Did you actually wire the electric cables together to turn on your Wi-Fi? Most likely not. The fact that you were able to just move your stuff inside your living space and live there is *incredible!*

Since adopting the practice of watching, tracking, and showing gratitude for my money, my bank account has only grown! Even without initially increasing my income (which came later down the road), extra money would just show up from unexpected sources. To this day, my bank account still gets larger and larger than the month before.

The principles I share *really* work. They're laws of the Universe, after all. Take ownership of your money, take care of it, show it love and respect, and money will take care of you in return.

Money Babe Action

1. Take the space below to write down notes while going through your bank accounts and credit card statements. Open up everything that pertains to your money, and use the space to keep track of what's going in, what's going out, and when:

2. Use this space below to show gratitude for your money. Which of your bills are you most grateful for? Which of your income sources are you most grateful for? How can you thank all the companies that are charging you for their incredible services that you have access to?

3. Use the space below to create your own little money tracking ritual. What do you plan to do when checking your bank balance every single day? Is it lighting a candle? Turning it into a dance party? Is it pouring yourself a glass of bubbly? The more fun you make this process, the more rewarding it will be.

Day Fifteen

The Money Is Already Manifesting

Congratulations on owning your shit, girlfriend. Do you even understand how proud I am of you for doing the work that you did yesterday?

If you haven't yet already, give yourself a pat on the back. You did something so many people are afraid of. And whether or not it was a scary process for you, give yourself a ton of credit. You deserve to celebrate it, babe!

After yesterday's money babe action, you can probably guess where I'm going with today. That's right...tracking your money!

Today my main goal is to prove to you that you are *already* abundant and money is flowing freely into your life.

If you don't see this yet, it's time to open your eyes. When I did this exercise the first time, I realized that I was literally manifesting about $100 a day into my life from unexpected sources *every single day!* I was taking $100 for granted on a consistent basis. No wonder I always felt broke, more gifts from the Universe that I wasn't acknowledging.

My daily $100 manifesting came through so many random ways. It would come from my friends buying me lunch. My boyfriend surprising me with coffee. Finding pennies, nickels, dimes, dollars on the ground. Noticing a parking meter had time left over in it from the person who parked before me. Getting a discount at the register when purchasing something I was already going to buy, and being able to keep $20 in my pocket. The restaurant I was having dinner at comping me for a meal out of the blue.

I quickly realized that I was already abundant and money found its way into my life all the time. But, if I would've never thought to track the money coming into my life, I would have never realized that I was already manifesting so much on a daily basis.

It's so important to take note of the money coming into your life. So many people set a goal of manifesting $1,000 or more into their lives, just to realize that the money has been sitting right under their noses the entire time.

Your assignment is to spend the next 24 hours tracking your money. Open up a spreadsheet, your journal, the "notes" app on your phone, or use the space below this chapter and start writing down all the money that comes your way.

Found a penny on the ground? Write it down.
Friend bought your coffee? Write it down.
Saved $0.30 on a gallon of gas? Write it down.

Remember that the more you feel abundant, the more abundance will flow your way. The more money you acknowledge, the more of it flows your way. The Universe responds to your vibration. You have to *be* the person who has an extra $1,000 in their life. How would someone who manifested $1,000 act?

If you had $1,000 in your hand right now, what would your posture be like? Would you stand up straight for once? Would you smile? Would you get your nails done? Maybe go get a massage? Get rid of clothing that's ripped and should've been in the trash months ago?

Would you speak with more confidence?

When you *act* like the person who has all the money in the world, the Universe responds. The Universe will give you exactly what you already are. Your reality is just an illusion that you create. So why create anything less than incredible? Anything less than absolutely amazing? *Why the hell not?*

I want to encourage you to start dreaming bigger because you can literally have, be, do, and create *anything* you want.

Say it with me: Money is an unlimited resource. It is always flowing my way.

Repeat it a thousand times and watch the channels of abundance open up!

Money Babe Action

Use the space below as a record of all the money that is already manifesting into your life:

1. What was the total amount of money that you received today?

_____

_____

_____

_____

Notes:

Day Sixteen

Up Your Value, Up Your Income

When people increase their value, they become money magnets.

Here's what's backwards in our society: People believe that rich people are born rich, and thus they are valuable because they are rich. They look at others who have a higher income, and automatically think that is what makes them valuable. But it's not. That's not how it works. It's the fact that they're so valuable that their income is so high. They started by adding value into the world, and their incomes grew as a result.

Everyone is born onto the same level playing field. Those who add value to the world, and *feel* like they are valuable, are the ones who become rich. This is why the playing field is level no matter how humble some of our beginnings are.

Today is all about increasing your value in order to increase your pay. Wouldn't it be amazing to go beyond manifesting $1,000? To permanently and consistently keep increasing your income so that it never falls back to a level that no longer serves you? An income level that makes you feel secure, free, happy, supported, and in love with life?

How does that sound to you?

Really good, right? Perfect!

It is a known principle that when you increase your value, your income increases as an effect. More value, more money! This concept is pretty obvious when we compare it to luxury cars.

Why do we want the Mercedes or the BMW over the Honda or Toyota? They're all just cars anyway right? However, we tend to value the luxury cars over the more practical ones for a reason. They hold some kind of value to us, whatever it may be.

Is it the leather seats? The fancy headlights? The brand name itself? The smoother ride? The service we get at the dealership? It varies from person to person, but my point is that there is a price gap between the two. The price gap is determined by the value we place on the luxury cars vs. the more practical cars.

We often choose what we value, and today's assignment is all about choosing to value yourself while learning how to increase your value that you put out into the world.

How do we increase our value? Step one is to see and believe yourself to be valuable. If you don't see yourself as valuable, then who will? Realize that you are *already* so valuable. You are so unique. You possess gifts, talents, and abilities that no one else in the entire universe has. No one can do things the way that you do. When you were created, you were created with a purpose to come on to this planet and impact people's lives like *no one* else can. You are one among *billions*. You possess something that over 7 billion people do not have! How freaking cool is that? So, you are *already* incredibly valuable. You just don't see it yet. My job to help you prove it to yourself.

For today's money babe action, I want you to list 15 things you value about yourself, what makes you unique, what makes you stand out, what you bring into the world (including your friends, your family, etc.) and any accomplishments or achievements you're proudest of. Fifteen is the minimum but I promise you that those with high incomes can list *at least* 100+. And they are no more special than you.

Go big here! What makes you valuable, babe?

A few examples to get you started:

1. I graduated from college
2. I can make people laugh in any circumstance
3. I am able to motivate and inspire my clients and therefore they are drawn to me
4. I raised a child as a single mother
5. I built my business completely from scratch and it generates me enough of an income to provide for me and my family

There are five I came up with as examples off the top of my head for someone who sounds like an amazing person, right? This should be easy for you. It's fun. It makes you feel amazing. And remember… money is drawn to those who feel really good about themselves! Money is a magnet to those who value themselves.

Money Babe Action

Go for it, girlfriend. Start impressing the shit out of yourself:

1.

_____

2.

_____

3.

_____

4.

_____

5.

_____

6.

_____

7.

_____

8.

_____

9.

_____

10.

_____

11.

_____

12.

_____

13.

_____

14.

_____

15.

_____

Now that you've listed your 15, I bet you feel pretty damn valuable, don't you?

Now how do we increase our value even more? How do we increase our incomes based on the value we put out into the world?

Become a student of life. Start growing. Start reading books. Start going to seminars. Join a workshop to expand your knowledge on a topic that interests you. Take some classes. Start listening to podcasts aimed at successful people. Start doing what other successful people do. Listen to what they listen to. Adopt habits of successful people.

Doing all of this will give you the confidence that you need in your areas of expertise. Make it so there's no freaking way people wouldn't pay you lots of money to share your knowledge with the world! This is how you become a natural money magnet. Stop hiding your gifts, talents, abilities, and other unique things about you from everyone. It's those very things that will make you rich.

Your $1,000 plus soooooo much more is already yours. Keep upping your value and you'll keep upping your income.

Money Babe Action

List below 10 ways that you can become a student of life, invest in yourself, and up your value in the world to become a money magnet.

1.

_____

_____

_____

2.

_____

_____

_____

3.

4.

5.

6.

7.

8.

9.

10.

Day Seventeen

Squashing Limiting Beliefs

Hey gorgeous soul, I have a question for you: Do you desire to become insanely rich? A millionaire? A billionaire, perhaps? Live a life of freedom, be able to cruise down to the Caribbean on the regular with your family, open up a charity, and retire your parents?

Yes? But what about that little voice in your head that keeps repeating "rich people are greedy" in your head? What about the voice that keeps saying "you have to be a slave to money in order to earn enough of it?"

Today is the day that we knock out some, if not all, of your limiting beliefs around money. As a mindset coach, I *looooooove* doing this work with my clients.

You see, consciously we are aware of what's going on. We *know* we have a crazy story around money. We can damn well see that it's taking its toll on our finances. But subconsciously? We can't stop seeing money as dirty. We heard our entire lives that rich people are greedy and money is hard to earn, so therefore we don't want to become slaves and there's no way in hell we want to be labeled as greedy!

So, we remain stuck. This is when self-sabotage kicks in. We consciously strive for more money, but somehow "miss the boat" when it comes to receiving it. Sucks, doesn't it?

What if I told you there's an easy fix to this? In fact, what if I told you I can help you eliminate a limiting belief in under 20 minutes? I have a clear written out limiting-belief-squashing step-by-step process that I regularly take myself and my clients through if we ever come across any resistance to money.

Limiting beliefs can be right in front of our noses, or they can be hidden really deep inside of us. The thing to remember about limiting beliefs is that they are just beliefs that limit us in some way, shape, or form. They hold us back from taking action. They are the reason we procrastinate. They are the reason we never grow the balls to make the phone call, to get in front of a potential client, to get up on stage, to quit our jobs, and to start a business.

Beliefs are just thoughts that we keep thinking to ourselves over and over again. In order to change the belief, we must find the source, or initial thought, and consciously replace it with a new thought. This new thought is the opposite thought that we find to be way more empowering and freeing. Then, all we have to do is to turn the new empowering thought into an empowering belief.

All that limiting beliefs are, are just stories. These stories are a bunch of bullshit fed to us by someone else, or society in general, at some point in our lives. Start telling yourself a new story, and your reality will begin to reflect the new story. It's truly as simple as that.

The 8 Step Process To Squashing Any Limiting Belief

1. Identify the limiting behavior that's holding you back. Are you procrastinating? Hesitating? Afraid of taking action? Self-sabotaging?

2. Isolate the underlying limiting belief. What do you have to believe to be true in order to keep repeating the same limiting behavior?

3. Go back in time and find when you first developed the thought that led to your belief. Did you see something as a child? Did someone tell you something? Did you experience something that you assumed was the way that the world worked? What is the source of this belief?

4. Ask yourself what the benefits have been of holding onto this belief. How has holding onto this belief served you? Trust me, it is serving you in some way if you keep believing it. We need to uncover this.

5. Ask yourself what the consequences have been of holding onto this belief. What have you missed out on because of this belief? How painful are these consequences to you and how ready are you to change?

6. Is there any ultimate truth to this belief? Or is it just a story? Find as many reasons as you can to prove to yourself the falsehood of your limiting belief. Dig into your experiences for this and see what you can dig out.

7. What would the Universe, God, whatever you believe in, tell you about this belief? Can you see how this belief is doing nothing but limiting you from living your truth? From aligning with your divine abundance and money flow? What is the actual truth about this?

8. Choose a new thought and create a new story that empowers you. Formulate a new belief based on your answers from #7. Start acting as if you believe your new beliefs. Your subconscious doesn't know the difference between make believe and actual reality. To your subconscious, everything is reality. The new reality that you choose *will* manifest before you know it!

To help you get a clear idea of how I use this limiting-belief- squashing process, here is an example of one of my biggest limiting beliefs around money that I had around the time that I started to do major money mindset work.

1. *Limiting behavior :* Working nonstop, about 18 hours a day, feeling like if I stopped working the money flow would just stop.

2. *Limiting belief :* Money only comes from hard work and struggle.

3. *The source :* I remember watching my parents struggle, working nonstop to support us as a young immigrant family. I kept hearing the phrase, "if you work *really* hard, you will be successful" over and over again. This thought played on repeat and eventually became a belief. I ended up only receiving money from hard work and struggle.

4. *The benefits :* The benefits of holding onto this belief are that it would always keep me productive. I will always feel like I need to keep working, and thus I will get a lot of shit done.

5. *The consequences :* The consequences of this belief is that I will encounter burnout long before I even make the kind of money that I want. In fact, I am already experiencing burnout and I am tired of working. Not only am I still broke, but I'm tired too. I feel lost and exhausted. I am missing out on all of the fun in life, and I am just over it.

6. *Ultimate truth or just a story?* This is definitely a story. I have watched some of my friends earn money by doing really easy work, working only 20 hours a week. I have run into online entrepreneurs who earn most of their money through passive income. I have heard of

investors who live off of their investments, travel around the world, and hardly work hard at all! I can see how there is no truth in my limiting belief.

7. *The perspective of the Universe :* The Universe would tell me to start detaching work from money. The Universe would tell me to slow down and be purposeful with my work. I am a child of God, and deserve all the abundance in the world. Money doesn't come from hard work. It's a flow of energy that we just need to tune into, and attract into our lives. Money comes through the value we put out in the world. The truth is that money is an unlimited resource that's always flowing my way. I can choose to work hard, or hardly work at all. I will keep receiving money no matter what because I am already infinitely valuable to the world.

8. *The new thought or truth :* Money is an unlimited resource that is always flowing my way through expected and unexpected channels regardless of how many hours of work I put in.

Do you see how this process works? It's actually so easy to reframe every single story we keep telling ourselves as soon as we figure out the source.

Want a fun update? It's been two entire years since I worked through this limiting belief. At the time, I was working literally 18 hour days, drowning in $25,000 in debt, and making about $400 a week. *Clearly,* the time for money exchange was already a little out of whack here!

Today, I spend about 2-3 hours a day working (seeing clients, creating new content for *www.manifestationbabe.com*) and earn over $200,000 of my monthly income as *passive* income. I work significantly less, yet I have never been more financially free. The "hours worked = money earned" equation was a complete fluke. It was just a rule that I created for myself that manifested into my reality.

This shit really works. Eliminate what's holding you back, and your life takes shape around the new story you create. It's not magic, it's manifesting.

Use the space below to take yourself through my limiting-belief- squashing process. You can repeat this process on as many limiting beliefs that you hold around money as needed, but for today, let's just focus on one big one.

Money Babe Action

Sometimes it helps to meditate beforehand to identify what it is that we need to work through. Feel free to give yourself 10 minutes to relax and listen to your gut.

1. The limiting behavior that's holding you back:

_____

_____

_____

2. The underlying limiting belief that's related to the behavior:

_____

_____

3. The source of the belief:

4. Benefits of holding onto the belief:

5. Consequences of holding onto the belief:

6. Is this the ultimate truth? How can we find examples of falsehood behind this belief?

_____

_____

_____

7. What is the actual truth about money as it pertains to the falsehood of the belief?

_____

_____

_____

8. The new thought based on #7 that you choose to believe instead and create a new empowering story from.

_____

_____

9. How do you feel after working through your biggest limiting belief around money?

_____

_____

_____

10. How does it feel to uncover the real truth and create a new reality based on that?

_____

_____

_____

11. What is the new truth that you are committed to creating?

_____

_____

_____

12. How does this new truth feel to you?

_____

_____

_____

Notes:

Day Eighteen

Scripting

Before we begin today, I want to take a second and let you know how much I appreciate you. Do you know how incredible you are for sticking with this for almost *three weeks?* You are serious about changing your money mindset, and if I could take a wild guess, I would say that you have already been experiencing crazy shifts in your life.

Perhaps, money is flowing more than it ever has before. Maybe you already manifested your $1,000. Maybe you've manifested more than that! I am so fucking proud of you. Keep up the incredible work, girlfriend.

If you haven't yet seen the shifts, don't freak out! We still have work to do together. There's still so much fun to be had. We're about to do one of my favorite manifesting exercises, *like ever.*

If I were to take a magic wand right now, and wave it over your life, what would the perfect day in your life look like?

Today's money babe action is going to be really fun and powerful.

We're gonna do an assignment today that's called "scripting." Just like movie script writers script out their movies long before the movie is ever produced, we're going to script out your life before it manifests into reality....*so that it can become your reality.*

Grab a cup of tea, or coffee, a pen that feels luxurious to write with and start writing down what your perfect day would look like from the very second you open your eyes, to the second you close them at the end of the night. Don't forget to mention how you manifested the $1,000 so quickly and so easily that day.

You want to make sure that you write down your perfect day in the past tense.

Why past tense? Your subconscious mind accepts something as truth much faster when you write it down as if it happened in the past tense, rather than the present or future tense. Usually, when we start writing things down as if they're happening right now, our minds automatically flash "Liar! You're telling lies!" We want to trick our minds here. Therefore, we're gonna act like the day already happened.

To get some of your imaginative juices flowing, here are questions that you can answer to help you script out as many details as possible:

- Where did you wake up?

- What kind of bed is your perfect bed?

- What do the sheets feel like?

- What's the weather like on your perfect day?

- Who did you wake up next to?

- What did you have for breakfast?

- What was your morning ritual?

- What did you do for work today?

- What's your perfect career?

- How much did your clients pay you today?

- How much did you earn today if your income today was your perfect income?

- Do you have children?

- Do you have any pets to take care of?

- Where do you live?

- What kind of car do you drive?

- Did you travel anywhere today?

- How was lunch?

- How was dinner?

- How many times over did you manifest $1k?

- Did you go shopping? If so where?

- Did you meditate? Go to yoga class? Did you work out?

- What did you do for fun?

- What do you look like?

- What's your idea of perfect health?

- Who did you hang with?

- What time did you go to bed?

Get the point?

Script out your perfect day in the past tense as if your day just ended and you're reflecting back on it. That's the point of view I want you to have. And don't forget to *dream really big*. Remember it's your *perfect* day. I expect nothing less than incredible things from you, girl. You know better than to sell yourself short! Now get to scripting!

Money Babe Action

Use the space below to write out your perfect day as if it just ended. This is the exact kind of day that you will be manifesting into your reality. We must first define what we want before it manifests through Law of Attraction.

Day Nineteen

Where The Money Comes From

Often, I come across women who believe that the only way they will earn more money is if people decide to pay them more money. There is a strong connection between money and other people.

But Kathrin, what if I'm in a position where my only money sources come from other people? Doesn't it depend on them to want to give more money to me to receive my $1,000?

Here's the truth about where money comes from: **Money comes from the Universe** *through* **other people.**

Yes, other people are involved. Yes, people will have to buy your services. Yes, people will have to give you pay raises. Yes, people will have to hire you. But at the very energetic core? The money comes from the Universe. And the Universe won't keep your money from you. I promise.

However, we can work on appreciating all the amazing people in our lives as we often forget to. Be honest with me. When's the last time you told someone you appreciate them? Like really went out of your way to tell them? Not just after they did something for you?

You have so many amazing people in your life right now that deserve recognition from you. Money loves appreciative people. People love appreciative people. Money comes from the Universe through other people. Are you making this connection now?

Today's money babe action is to send 10 people appreciation notes.

Yep, 10! Not because you expect money to come from them (c'mon you know better than that!), but because you want to make someone else's day today.

When you increase other people's vibes, they in turn, increase yours too. Life is way more fun when you're surrounded by high vibe people.

Make a list of 10 people you will go out of your way and thank for something today. It can be for something they did, or the simple fact that they are in your life, love you dearly, and occasionally put up with your shit.

The thank you notes can be sent through text message, email, Facebook messenger, over the phone, with the best being in person. Make sure you *truly, truly* mean it. Go beyond just saying thank you. Go above and beyond because the Universe always goes above and beyond for you by bringing these people into your life in the first place. These people are in our lives for a reason. It's time to appreciate that reason.

What you put out into the world, always comes back to you. But, don't let this be your sole motivation. Always strive to make people's day because you want to without expecting anything in return. Set out on your day to make people smile, and you'll be amazed at all the shifts that happen in your life when you do this. The world you look at will literally change before your eyes.

Last but not least, don't be surprised if your manifestations come into fruition today out of the blue. The energy of gratitude and appreciation contains magic.

Money Babe Action

Here is a list to keep you accountable while writing your notes. Ready, set, go:

1.

_____

2.

_____

3.

_____

4.

_____

5.

_____

6.

_____

7.

_____

8.

_____

9.

_____

10.

_____

Notes:

Day Twenty

The Magic 10/10/10 Rule

Remember when I told you in the beginning of this book to just trust me and go with me? I'm gonna need more of that from you.

Especially today.

I want to share a principle I started to follow the day I decided to make money manifesting my bitch. The principle is called my "10/10/10 rule." It stands for "Save 10, Spend 10, Give 10.'

I'm pretty sure it came from half a book I read and half of my previous Christian background, but either way, it has worked *magic* in my life. It would be unfair for me to not put this rule in this book and keep its power from you. It could very well be the financial game changer for you too.

I have no background in finance, I'm no accountant, and I have yet to figure out exactly how I want to invest my money, but I *have* studied other prosperous people for a while now. One thing I've noticed is that the most prosperous people in the world follow certain prosperity rules. I'm no one to argue with proof, so I chose a percentage that made sense to me and went with it. 10/10/10 stands for percentages of money. Each percentage relates to where you allocate your money with each paycheck, payment, or source of income that you receive.

Every time you receive a paycheck, the first thing you would do is save 10% of it. That 10% is put into an untouchable savings account that you don't touch under any circumstance. The reason you don't touch it, is kinda obvious. You want your savings to grow before your eyes! This number's goal is to grow.

With the next 10%, donate it to a charity, church, or a cause that you believe in. Find someone or something that speaks to you (feel free to ask for Universal guidance! I do it all the time) and donate 10% of your money to them.

Tony Robbins, one of my biggest mentors, said something that stuck hardcore with me when I attended one of his seminars. He said "if you can't give away a dollar out of every 10, then you'll never be able to give away $100,000 out of every million." Wow, so true.

In order to ever get comfortable giving, you must start now. It becomes a habit. I see so many people get stuck in their own ways claiming they would love to donate money but will start doing so once they get wealthy. Not realizing, that the habit of donating on the regular is one of the things that lead wealthy people to their prosperity. There is just something powerful in financially blessing others. And the coolest part? The Universe blesses you 10x in return. *Always*. Like clockwork. Just wait till you see for yourself.

The final 10%? Spend that 10% on some fun stuff for yourself. Yep, I'm giving you permission to buy the purse, the shoes, and the diamond earrings you've been eyeing every time you walk into the mall. Spend 10% of your income on anything that makes you feel really abundant. Feeling abundant = Continuation of the money flow. When you deny yourself treats every now and then, the Universe will respond and deny *you* things in return. Not because you're unloved or unworthy, but because that's the vibration you're putting out. Whatever vibe you put out comes back to you.

Put out a vibe of scarcity or lack, and that's the vibe you get back.

So what about the rest of the money? Obviously, we need to pay our bills and eat. Use the rest of your money once the 10/10/10 allocation is done for bills, necessities, etc. If you have extra left over, save it! Get comfortable with having money in your account! It's really fun to watch it grow.

Babe, don't be afraid to be abundant with money. Be smart, but be abundant. Money is an unlimited resource and it is always flowing your way. Did you know that at any point in time there are *trillions* of dollars floating around you? Yes, trillions. Who says that a few thousand, hundreds of thousands of even millions of dollars can't float your way? Give it direction and it will come.

Next time you receive your paycheck, give the 10/10/10 rule a try. This will be your money babe action. I still use this money allocation principle to this day. You're hearing it from a girl who went $25,000 in debt earning $400 a week to financially free and earning over six figures a month in her own business in just one year.

Repeat after me: The more I give, the more I receive. The more I receive, the more I give. Money is an unlimited, renewable resource, and it fucking loves me.

#Boom.

Notes:

Day Twenty-one

Faith Is Like Wi-Fi

If it isn't already obvious to you, you can tell that the work we are doing together isn't just about money. It's about money, but really it extends far beyond dollar bills and numbers in your bank account.

Over the last three weeks we have been doing some incredibly powerful, energy-shifting work.

We have shifted some of your most deep-seated limiting beliefs around money, learned new money truths that serve you, and completely re-created and rescripted your money story. For the last day of the Money Babe challenge, I want to take a sec and talk about faith.

As you have already learned, money manifesting requires a lot of faith in the not yet seen. It requires us to believe in not only ourselves, but invisible forces that govern the way the planets spin so perfectly on their axes. The same forces that make grass grow, ensure that flowers bloom every single spring, and that the sun comes up every single morning day after day, are the forces that ensure that you are one abundant badass money attracting babe.

Faith is the difference maker when it comes to manifesting. It's the difference between walking around as a victim to staying broke, and actually opening up your eyes and seeing that money is already all around you. Just like you rely on your laptop or phone to connect to the Wi-Fi using invisible forces and waves coming out of the router, you need to start relying on yourself to connect with invisible Universal forces through faith.

Whether or not you have already manifested your $1,000 (which I have *zero* doubts that you already have), I want you to remember to keep the faith that your reality *will* match your new money mindset. It's not a bunch of magic fairy pixie dust magic. *It's law.* There is no other option for it, but to work.

In case you need a reminder on the basics of manifesting

1. Get really *really* clear on what you want. Intend for it to happen.

2. Believe without a shadow of a doubt that you can have it.

3. Eliminate all the reasons why it won't work or that you can't have it.

4. Believe to your very core the new truth you decide to tell yourself about why it will work.

5. Detach from the "how" it's going to happen.

6. Receive it like the money babe you know you are.

The Universe is always working its ass off on your behalf. Honor that and do your part by holding the faith that your money is already on its way to you. You are already the richest, happiest, most fulfilled, badass version of yourself. *So start acting like it.*

Today on our last day together, your final money babe action is to write a thank you note to the Universe. Or God. Or your angels. Whatever you believe in. It doesn't matter. Whoever it is to, make sure to make it *epic*.

You can thank the Universe for the $1,000 you had no idea would manifest when you first started this challenge, but did. You can thank the Universe for the fact that you even came across a book like this in the first place that radically transformed your money mindset when you most needed it. You can thank the Universe for the very fact that you are breathing right now, have eyes to see this page, and live on a beautiful planet as glorious as planet Earth.

Money Babe Action

Here is a place to do it right now. No excuses!

"Dear Universe,

Thank you SO much for

_____

_____

_____

_____

_____

_____

_____

_____

_____

Massive love,

(Your Name)

You have so much to be thankful for, gorgeous. You really do. Your money journey has just begun.

Feel free to manifest $1,000 all over again. Feel free to manifest $10,000, $100,000, or $1,000,000. The principles and the rules to manifest bigger amounts are exactly the same as the smaller amounts. There is no difference, nor does the Universe even care how much you choose.

The Universe is always saying yes. No matter what you ask for, the answer is always yes.

So ask big.

Notes:

Thank you so much for coming along on this incredible 21-day journey with me. I truly hope you had as much fun as I did. May you now see that manifesting money is possible, it can be done, and it's freaking easy. Feel free to come back and repeat the 21-day process at any time, or pick and choose your favorite exercises and do them as often as needed.

Shifting your money mindset isn't something that you work on just once. It's something you live, breathe, and eat. It takes work. It takes energy, but it's the best damn project you will ever work on.

Cheers to manifesting endless amounts of money, Money Babe.

To Your Massive Success
Kathrin Zenkina
Master Mindset Coach
Creator of Manifestation Babe
www.ManifestationBabe.com

Extra Writing Space

Workbook Success Stories

1. Amazing things will Happen. I am so grateful for this book!

I was skeptical when I bought this book but I truly had nothing to lose. I really wanted to start changing my mindset. So before the book, my kids, husband and I had been living with family. We were trying to buy a house (in escrow actually) but things we're not looking good for our funding (long story).

Day two of the book was a hard one for me and I actually put it off because I didn't want to rehash negative feelings; however, once I did it I felt a huge shift in my mind and body. The day after I did it I got a call that our funding would be fine and we were closing a few days later! I was shocked! Happy and scared.

So then I kept doing the book every day, I was feeling happier already. I was talking to my husband about needing a new computer for school and about stuff I wanted to do for the house. At the same time our second car had broken down too. Of course, I was worried about money to do it all. He kept saying "we will be fine", later I got it out of him that he was getting a bonus check at work. I figured like $300 or something like that....

Day 8 I kid you not was when amazing things happened! We got the keys to our house! And his bonus deposited in our account. It was $4500 and I was shocked! I was able to buy my new computer and paint that day. Then the next day we found out we would be getting our total good faith deposit back $1500!

Then the next day I received notice my credit card limit was increase by $150. My cousin was also able to fix our car enough to get it running.

With moving I have only gotten to day 14 but after having $6,150 come into my life ($4700 completely unexpected) I am a believer and I'm still in shock. This stuff doesn't happen to me ever lol I feel so blessed and happy. I know more abundance is coming our way too. I wanted to share so all of you could be inspired to keep going.

~ Natalie

2. Think. Believe. Achieve!!

I finished my first ever 21-day challenge yesterday and am so excited I wanted to share my story. So my goal was to manifest $5,000 in 21 days and I ended up manifesting $8,469 for which I am so grateful!!

On my first day I was telling my wife about what I was doing and had literally just finished saying to her that I believe that I can easily manifest $5,000 in 21 days, when I looked down and saw a 5c coin on the ground. I was super grateful and blown away by how quickly my words had manifested. For me it was a personal sign that I was on the right track.

My next universe moment was when I was thinking in my head about a situation that had just happened that I was extremely grateful for, as soon as I had said thank you to the universe I look down and there is another 5c coin (5 is my lucky number). During my newly learnt Forgiveness Ritual, I was forgiving a man from my past whom I lost $18,000 to which turned out to be scam. After 10+ years I forgave the situation (haven't heard from him since then) and then I get an email from him later that day asking if I wanted to invest in a new project. Of course, I declined and removed myself from his mailing list but I was just so blown away by how the forgiveness ritual that Kathrin Zenkina teaches is soooo powerful!

Another Universe moment happened for me today, which I set in motion on the first day of my challenge. During my clean out of my office, car and wallet, I decided to buy myself a new wallet to honor my money better so it wasn't being folded up. I ordered a great wallet from the states (San Francisco) knowing that it would take a while to get here (Australia), and sent myself a note with it congratulating me on manifesting $5,000. Today, it turns up!!!

So, my money ended up coming from all different sources which I would have never have found had I not done this challenge. Some came from lost government money that I chased up, some from my self-published book that I sent to a distributor years before that I had forgotten all about, and some I found while clearing out my spaces.

I ended up watching each video in the challenge twice per day, and then the podcast twice a day as well to literally brainwash myself. I would listen in the car on the way to the gym, driving around, in front of my computer etc etc.

I have learnt and changed so much in this course, it is so much more than just money, for me it has truly been life changing. Kathrin Zenkina you are an absolute gem, I am forever grateful for your teachings.

And today...I start my 21-day adventure again, but this time my goal is $15,000. All the best to all the Babes, think believe achieve!!

~ Nathan

3. Manifestation testimony

I'm that girl that wrote a FB post about being disappointed that my 21-day challenge didn't work, that I had a $7000 medical bill and that whole thing. Well, my goal was to manifest about $8000 with the challenge. By the time, I made that post I had manifested about $1000 dollars. Far from what I needed. As of right now I have manifested over $10,000!!!! (Not counting my regular paychecks.) all of a sudden, the money started coming in. I'm a nanny, and my boss gave me a Christmas bonus 10x bigger than she has ever given to me before.

I started getting random calls to do babysitting for other families, I started doing Doordash here and there, I got a $5,800 discount on my medical bill. I got checks for Christmas, and I'm not even including the actual presents. Got discounts, huge discounts everywhere.

And yesterday when I stopped to do the math, I have reached over $10,000!! And I just can't believe it!! I'm so blessed and so thankful for you guys for not letting me give up! It is possible people, and I needed to share this with you!! Just keep going and believing

~ Ana

4. This journey has been so liberating

This is my third time going through 'Unleash Your Inner Money Babe' and it is seriously changing everything for me. I have always been so afraid of looking at my money story for so long. This journey has been so liberating and I know that it is only the beginning. In the last three months I have:

-Moved into a new beautiful, high vibe af home

-Started working at the #1 spa in my city

-invested in myself and got a coach that I completely admire and look up to

-Finally made the decision to step into Life Coaching myself!

-Have manifested a beautiful, divinely romantic heart connection

-Not to mention the financial abundance flowing in from every direction currently!!

And I know this is just the beginning! I am done being afraid of being seen and allowing the fears and doubts to hold me back from taking INSPIRED ACTION.

I no longer work just to work. I work to kick ass and LIVE for a living!

~ Katie

5. I'm on day 7 of Kathrin Zenkina's UYIMB and I have to tell you a story because it's AMAZING!!!

On one of the Money Babe Actions we are told to write 5 things that make us happy when we have the time to do them. I wrote out 1-4 easily and for #5 I had to think a little harder. And I thought, "duh", plan our wedding. We've been engaged for a year and a half and because 2 babies and 1 house later, the wedding is on the back burner. We actually just saw our first venue two weeks ago to get the ball rolling...

The following question asks which of the 5 stands out the most. I almost wrote down my #3, but instead wrote down #5 because it felt stronger in the moment. The very last doodle I made states, "MANIFEST the money for the wedding".

The very next day after doing this action I got a phone call. Actually, my dad and I have been playing phone tag for 2 days. We chatted for 10 minutes and then he tells me the "real reason he called".

He wants to give us $5k to start planning our wedding. WHAAAAAAAAT? This is the same man who has told me since I was 10 that he never believed the bride's parents should fund a "big party", so not to expect that. He was so against it.

My first thought? "The universe literally just aligned this to actually happen?!" Then I knew exactly why this happened as soon as the words came out of his mouth. Like, I sort of wasn't even shocked 2 seconds later.

I'm so excited to finish this workbook and keep shifting my mindset, because it's so fun and totally works!!! (Just in case you've ever doubted) Thanks for reading my kickass story!

~ Jessica

Resources

To find out more about manifesting your dream reality and accessing every single freebie resource I've ever put out for Manifestation Babe, visit ***www.manifestationbabe.com/freebies***

In the resource library on my website, you will find an affirmation guide, a vision board training, guided meditations, worksheets, cheat sheets and workbooks that can help you expand on some of the lessons shared in this book.

I would also encourage you to check out Start Here page ***www.manifestationbabe.com/start-here*** which will give you a step by step guide on how to get started on manifesting the life of your dreams!

Looking for your dose of manifestation inspiration? With over 1,000 5-star reviews and over 1 million downloads, 100% of listeners agree that the Manifestation Babe podcast is their favorite way to feed their minds and start their day. Best of all? It's 100% free and available on Apple podcasts and Spotify. Visit ***www.manifestationbabe.podbean.com***

If you feel called to join one of my academies, sign up for one of my digital courses, or go to my retreat in Bali, you can find more information at *www.ManifestationBabe.com*

Have a testimonial to share with me? Have questions you want to ask me? I pop into my Facebook group, Manifestation Babes, on a regular basis. This is my favorite way to interact with you! I would love to see you there.

Join MB community of over 55,000 empowering, uplifting and positive women by requesting an invite through the link below *www.facebook.com/groups/manifestationbabesgroup* or simply by searching "Manifestation Babes" in the group search bar on Facebook. (Please read group rules before sending us a request.)

Also, be sure to follow me on Instagram at **@ManifestationBabe** to stay up to date with even more tips on mindset, money, and manifesting.

Made in the USA
Monee, IL
17 November 2023